Jane Brocket's CLEVER CONCEPTS

Spiky, Slimy, Smooth

What Is TEXTURE?

M

Millbrook Press · Minneapolis

Touch your nose.
How does it feel?

The way something
feels is called
TEXTURE.

Let's look around to
see what textures
we can find.

Furry slippers are **soft and fluffy**. They tickle your toes and keep your feet warm.

What else is **soft and fluffy**? How about layers of soft, sweet cake and frosting? They feel **light and spongy** when you eat them.

Jam is **sticky and gooey**. It is easy to spread on toast. But it stays on your fingers until you lick it off. Mmmmm...

You can feel things with your feet too. Have you ever felt mud between your bare toes? It is **gooey** and **very oooooozy.**

Old flower heads are **dry and papery**. Rub them between your fingers. They crumble into little flakes.

Cookies sprinkled with sugar feel **dry** too. The sugar makes the ridges on top stand out. You can see them as well as feel them.

Cactus plants are **spiky and sharp.** They aren't nice to touch.

Pebbles and stones can be sharp and pointy too. It's much easier to walk on them in shoes than with bare feet.

Candy wrappers are **smooth and shiny**. They make a rustling sound when you scrunch them up.

A watermelon has a thick, smooth skin. It protects the juicy fruit inside.

DELICIOUS & NUTRITIOUS
A two cup serving of watermelon is an excellent source of vitamins A, B6 and C.
WATERMELONS

Look at all these different squash! Some are plain and smooth. Some are knobbly and warty. And some are curvy and lumpy.

15

Oil is greasy and wet. It makes these tomatoes slippy and slidy.

Raw eggs are **wobbly and runny and slimy**. They feel very funny.

Just-picked fruits and vegetables taste fresh and crisp.

Apples are **firm and crunchy**. An apple makes a loud noise when you bite into it. Lettuce feels **light and crinkly** and easy to eat.

Freshly fallen snow can be **crisp and crunchy** under your boots. But if you catch a snowflake on your tongue, you can feel how light and cold it is.

Things made from metal feel **hard**. When we hold them, they don't bend or change shape.

Tiles are also hard. They are smooth and cool to touch. But the thin gaps between tiles feel gritty and rough.

At home, we have **soft, squishy** textures to keep us warm.

On winter days, it's nice to snuggle under woolly blankets and stitched cotton quilts.

What else is nice to touch? Apricots and peaches are **fuzzy and dry.**

If you could hold a butterfly,
it might feel soft and
dusty and very
fluttery.

Some things are not so nice to touch. These scrubbing brushes are **bristly and scratchy.**

Bricks and stones are **hard and rough**. They might scrape your knuckles and knees if you try to climb this wall.

27

Candies have lots of different textures.

Some are stretchy and rubbery. Some are smooth and melting. Some are crackly and crunchy.

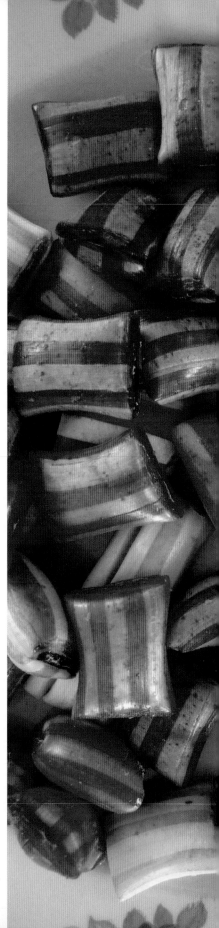

TEXTURE

is all around us.

Everything we touch has its own texture. Look and feel around you, and see what textures you can find. **What words would you use to describe them?**

Text and photographs copyright © 2011 by Jane Brocket

Millbrook Press
A division of Lerner Publishing Group, Inc.
241 First Avenue North
Minneapolis, MN 55401 U.S.A.

Website address: www.lernerbooks.com

Additional images in this book are used with the permission of: © iStockphoto.com/eliane (cardboard background); © iStockphoto.com/Winston Davidian (textured paper background).

Library of Congress Cataloging-in-Publication Data

Brocket, Jane.
    Spiky, slimy, smooth : what is texture? / text and photographs by Jane Brocket.
      p.   cm. — (Jane Brocket's clever concepts)
    ISBN: 978–0–7613–4614–2 (lib. bdg. : alk. paper)
    1. Touch—Juvenile literature. 2. Surfaces (Technology)—Juvenile literature. I. Title.
QP451.B75 2011
612.8'8—dc22   2010028933

Manufactured in the United States of America
1 – DP – 12/31/10

For Louis
and Charlotte
—J.B.

With many thanks
to Carol Hinz
and Danielle Carnito